W9-ARU-950

talking dogs

talking dogs

a celebration of the canine spirit

edited by sean keogh

Published in the United States in 2008
by Tangent Publications
an imprint of
Axis Publishing Limited
8c Accommodation Road
London NW11 8ED
www.axispublishing.co.uk

Creative Director: Siân Keogh
Designer: Simon de Lotz
Production Manager: Jo Ryan

ISBN 978-1-904707-82-0

9 8 7 6 5 4 3 2 1

Printed and bound in China

about this book

Talking Dogs brings together an inspirational selection of powerful, life-affirming, and humorous phrases written by dogs for dogs and their owners, combined with evocative and gently amusing photographs.

We all lead busy lives and sometimes forget to pause and appreciate how amusing, and inspirational, dogs can be. These examples of wit and wisdom sum up the pleasure of owning a dog and watching as it goes about its daily life.

A quick glance at this book will confirm why it is no wonder that dogs are still "man's (and women's) best friend."

about the author

Sean Keogh has worked in publishing for several years, on a variety of books and magazines covering a wide range of subjects. From the many hundreds of contributions that were sent to him from all over the world, he has selected those that best sum up what owning a dog is all about—the joys, the quirks and the new take on the world a dog offers.

I used to be dyslexic.

Take my advice—
I don't use it anyway.

The problem with being punctual is that there's never anyone around to appreciate it.

I don’t do junk food.

Fetch it yourself.

I will win this race.

Bacon, bacon, I smell bacon,
only one thing smells like bacon,
and that's BACON!

It's all a big show…

…I wouldn't really
bite the postman.

I refuse to apologize…

…it was only a small hole.

YOU threw it, why should
I have to go and get it?

It's not that I'm too long,
I'm just too short.

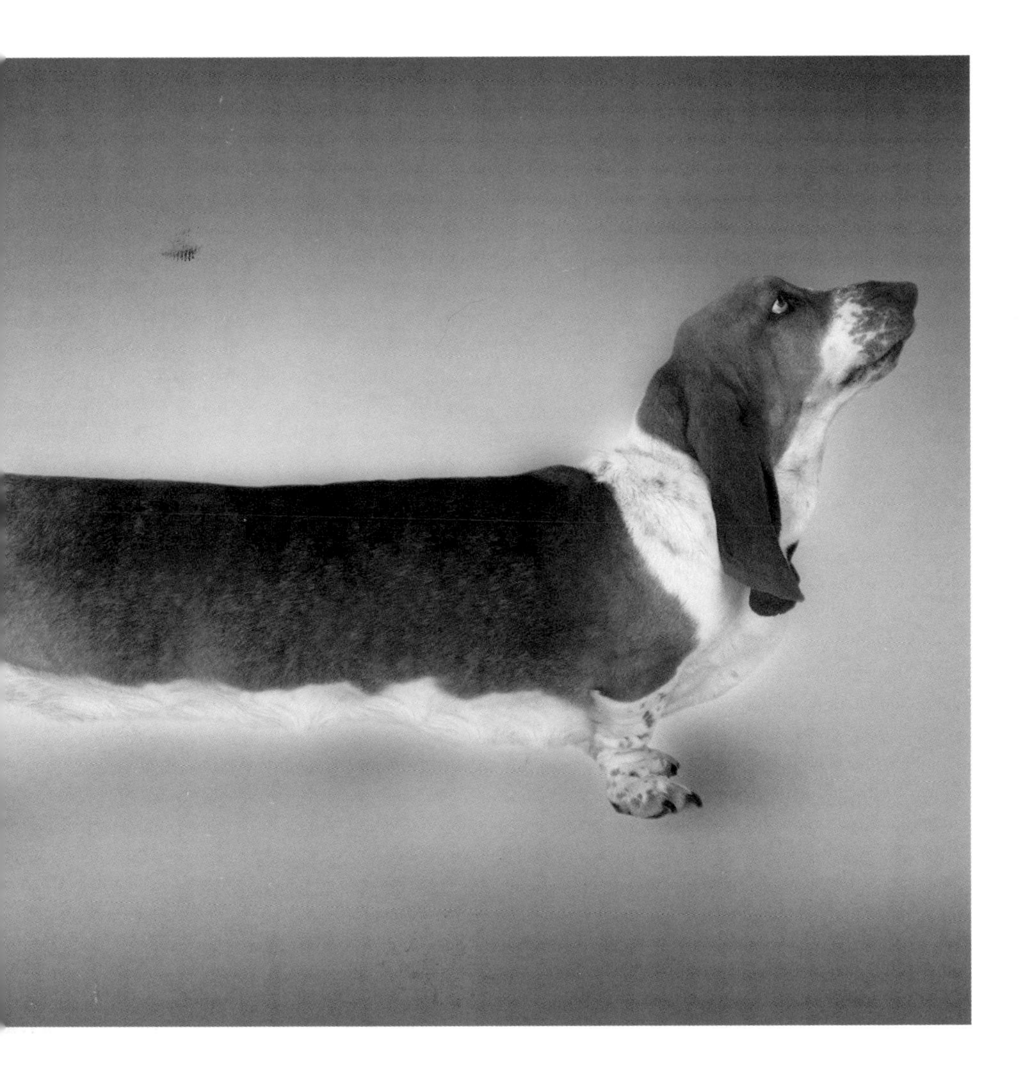

Why does everyone say
I look like batman?

A positive mental attitude will annoy enough people to make it worth the effort.

A procrastinator's work
is never done.

No human could ever love
you as much as I do.

Gotta catch the tail… gotta catch the tail… gotta catch the tail… gotta catch the tail… gotta.

The only way around
is through.

HANNOVER

You don’t own me…

…I own you.

Dogs don’t eat dogs.

Sleep with dogs, rise with fleas.

Opposites attract.

If I like it, it's mine.
If I saw it first, it's mine.
If it's in my paws, it's mine.
If it looks like mine,
it's mine.

Running helps the
ground to feel needed.

Only mad dogs and Englishmen
stay out in the midday heat.

When please doesn't work…

…beg.

Let sleeping dogs lie.

If your dog doesn't like someone you probably shouldn't either.

A dog makes a house a home.

Show a dog a finger,
and he wants the whole hand.

A good dog deserves a bone.

I have so many friends because I wag my tail, not my tongue.

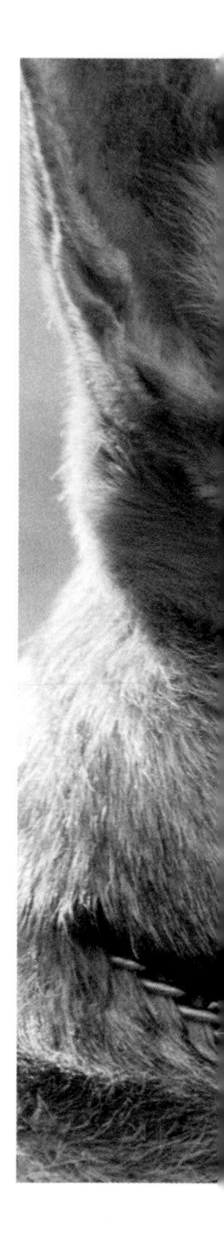

Tomorrow you can fetch
your own newspaper.

A thick skin is a gift from God.

Wonder is the
beginning of wisdom.

They thought I was brave…

…I just didn’t have the courage to run away.

You want me to follow?
You have to feed me first.

The journey is the reward.

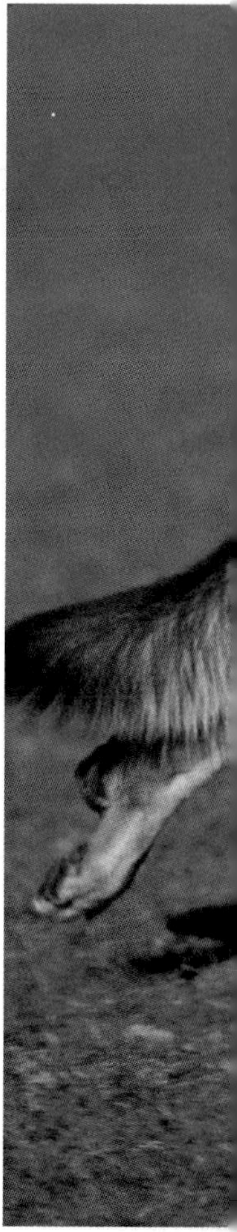

Look into my eyes…

…you WILL drop that food on the floor.

Always schedule in a nap.

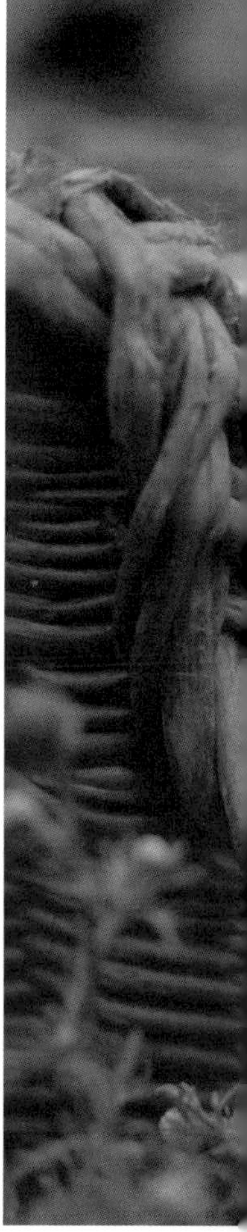

I may be getting fat…

…but you're not getting enough exercise.

Do not respond
to a barking dog.

Those who know the least,
obey the best.

You want me to jump
HOW high?

Friends Fur-ever.

The dog who does things that count, doesn't usually stop to count them.

Dogs are people too.

Every puppy needs a boy.

Listen to the silence.

I am a nobody, nobody is perfect,
therefore I am perfect.

One dog barks at something,
the rest bark at him.

Exercise: you don't have time not to.

A piece of grass a day
keeps the vet away.

A need is a want you
can't do without.

Nothing is foolproof to a
sufficiently talented fool.

You know which ever side
of the door I’m on, will be wrong.

Beware of a silent dog
and still waters.

Every dog may have his day—but it's the puppies that have the weekends.

If I stare at you for long enough…

…eventually you'll give in.

Next time you put a bow in my
hair I will chew your stuff
up when you are out.